# Face to Face Marketing

"ADirectMarketingSystem is asking a direct?
and awaiting a direct response"

ADirectMarketingSystem publication

# Face to Face Marketing

## What Your Mama Never Knew

BC Adamkowski

To order additional copies of this book, contact:
Xlibris Corporation
1-888-795-4274
www.Xlibris.com
Orders@Xlibris.com
88010

# 99 Direct Marketing Keys

1. Speak Vaguely
2. Look people in the eyes
3. Smile, and then some
4. Be peaceful
5. Offer something
6. Maintain eye contact
7. Speak clearly
8. Speak correctly
9. Speak with peace, confidence, and enthusiasm
10. Ask a direct question
11. Use hand gestures
12. Communicate clearly and concisely
13. Look the part
14. Stay warm
15. Think positively
16. Think lovingly
17. Keep an open head
18. Keep an open face
19. Be well groomed
20. Wear cologne
21. Brush your teeth
22. Fix your teeth
23. Use mints and mouthwash
24. Believe in value
25. Say hello
26. Initiate conversation
27. Engage people's interests
28. Love children
29. Pay attention to her
30. Ask their names and ages
31. Really be interested in them
32. Value people
33. Talk fab
34. Tell what it will do for them
35. Be joyful
36. Do not joke unless you are the butt
37. Blend like a chameleon
38. Think win/win
39. Make people feel good
40. Bless people
41. Be persistent
42. Maintain a good work ethic
43. Stay relaxed
44. Never sweat or fret
45. Detach emotionally from results
46. Work the numbers
47. Work the system
48. Ask for help
49. Say please
50. Say thank you
51. Don't work too hard
52. Give emotionally to people
53. Sow a loving, positive seed
54. See yourself as a specialist
55. Envision success
56. Develop success rituals
57. Laugh/ humor
58. Learn by experience
59. Never think you have arrived
60. Use giveaways
61. Be flexible

62. Stay loose
63. Think
64. Be a student of people
65. Listen
66. Use time efficiently
67. Assume consent
68. Reject rejection
69. Hyper extend emotions
70. Respond
71. Be well rested
72. Forget failure
73. Laugh at yourself
74. Remember faces
75. Go towards them
76. Expect success
77. Eat right
78. Move at their speed
79. Do not curse or use slang
80. Let them win
81. Be courteous and mannerly
82. Focus totally
83. Demonstrate
84. Play
85. Be thankful
86. Refuse discouragement
87. Work with urgency
88. Think others
89. Be gracious and endearing
90. Be gentle and respectful
91. Never quit
92. Detest complacency
93. Avoid self fulfilling prophecies
94. Work peak times
95. Be realistic
96. Hand pen
97. Display uniquely
98. Think marathon
99. Don't take it all so seriously

## 1. Speak vaguely

When it come to the art of generating fine, quality leads—vagueness works. Learn to speak in generalities. This will entice the listener for more information. Remember . . . say what you must to create more interest.

## 2. Look people in the eyes

Eye contact is a must. It creates a connection and intimacy with people. It also says you are honest and not afraid to look someone in the eye. Sincerity sells. Remember . . . maintaining eye contact creates confidence . . . in you and your prospect.

## 3.   Smile and then some

When working an event, realize what
you look like to other people. Learn
to smile some more. Look at yourself
in a mirror. See what you do look like.
You will be surprised. Smiles attract.
Remember . . . frowns repel.

## 4.   Be peaceful

The one thing people find irresistible is
a peaceful person. Remember to relax
and be at peace as you are talking to
your prospect. So many move so fast and
are not at peace. So if you can genuinely
be at peace, people will be attracted.
Shalom!

# 5. Offer something

Give and it shall be given to you . . . give or add something of value to your prospect. It is totally amazing how what we give will create currents of favor back to us. Remember . . . plant a seed and it can grow. Plant nothing, and reap nothing.

# 6. Maintain eye contact

The first hello is with our eyes and a warm open face. Create intimacy with continued eye contact. Many people won't do it. But when you sincerely look someone in the eye you are building rapport. You are saying they matter.

# 7.   Speak clearly

With all the slang and people from other countries it is imperative to speak clearly. Remember to enunciate your words and remember you do want the other person to understand what you are saying.

# 8.   Speak correctly

Ditto: #7. Enunciate and use every sound. "Walking", not "walkin". Choose grammatically correct words and phrases. Avoid ain't, can't—slang terms—ghetto terms.

## 9. Speak with peace and confidence

The tone and spirit you communicate with really can attract or repel. Remember Edith Bunker of "all in the family fame". It really does matter: listen to yourself on tape. Get to know "how" you sound to others!

## 10. Ask a direct question

Most people don't mind being solicited as long as you don't waste their time in doing it. Time. It is a precious commodity. Get down to it. Ask a direct question.

## 11. Use hand gestures

Think of a flight deck of an air carrier. Gestures mean something. Wave people over to you. Use your hands efficiently to entice your prospect. People will respond. Try it, you will be surprised. We all communicate visually!

## 12. Communicate clearly and concisely

When talking to prospects, get to the point. Use as few words as possible. Most people don't mind giving a quick yes or no answer. Just don't waste their time with a drawn out presentation. Time, value it, yours and others!

## 13. Look the part

Whatever you are promoting, it is
important to look the part. Sometimes
a suit, sometimes khakis and a sweater.
Remember the master marketer is a
chameleon. He blends in and looks the
part. So if you are selling horseshit, look
like . . . . smell like . . .

## 14. Stay warm

Communicate love, warmth, acceptance,
and non judgment to people you meet.
Be soft, gentle, courteous, nurturing,
caring, and loving. It is amazing what
this will do for you. We are all looking
for a good feeling. MAKE THOSE
MOMENTS FOR OTHERS!

## 15.  Think positively

This is the #1 quality you need to
succeed. Never let the thought "no one
is interested" cross your mind. Many will
not, some will. Hold the positive thought.
Remember someone is interested in what
you are offering. Besides you are totally
irresistible!

## 16.  Think lovingly

People go through life and get bruised
and beat up. When you act in a loving
manner people will respond to it.
Remember . . . everyone I meet is
entitled to a loving exchange. This makes
the world a better place.

## 17. Keep an open head

Just be. Exist. Have no judgments
or prejudices about people or your
day. Do your diligence to do your
task and success will accompany you.
Remember . . . today is a new day. Keep
your options open.

## 18. Keep an open face

Appearance is everything. Keep a warm,
open look on your face. Look at yourself
in a mirror. Sometimes our expressions
can be less than flattering. Even sad or
angry. Remember . . . people like to deal
with a warm, open face.

## 19. Be well groomed

This is really common sense yet again, a picture is worth a thousand words and you only have one chance to make a first impression. Hair cut, styles, shaved face or legs, look good, feel good, and good will come to you. Remember . . . casual can be well groomed.

## 20. Wear cologne

We appeal to others through sight, smell, touch, taste, and hearing, the five physical senses. Remember . . . smell good, wear cologne, wash, and be well groomed.

## 21. Brush your teeth

Again, we appeal to people
through the five physical senses.
Remember . . . nothing is worse than
bad breath or food stuck between your
teeth. Clean up or Shut up!

## 22. Fix your teeth

People are turned on or off by our
appearance. So if you need dental work,
do your best to get it done. It really
does matter what people think about
you.

## 23. Use mints and mouthwash

You just had lunch at the Olive Garden, soup and salad. Remember #21 and rinse your mouth and get some mints. This applies to smokers as well.

## 24. Believe in value

If you don't believe in the value of what you are offering, then quit and get another job. Value and adding value to your customers is what I believe to be the #1 tool needed to succeed in lead generation. If you ain't legit, quit!

## 25. Say hello

Make the first move. This is great if you are a bit introverted or shy. You can overcome it. Exposure brings healing and wholeness. Remember . . . say hello. You have something to offer the world. YOU!

## 26. Initiate conversation

Smile, eye contact, and hello are a good start. Success will come as you learn to reach out and touch someone in a positive way. Ask questions to initiate conversation and do it sincere and people will respond.

# 27. Engage peoples interests

Hats, shirts, and strollers are all
clues to what interest your prospect.
Talk about their interests. Avoid long
dissertations about you. Talk much about
Them.

F-Family

O—Occupation

R—Recreation

M—Money

These are all places to start engaging.

# 28. Love children

Jesus taught it. He knew something
about human nature. Sincerely learn
to love children. This is a way of favor
with prospects. But do it from the
heart . . . not as a technique or sale
gimmick. The truer to yourself that
you do, the more you will shine through.
Sincerely love children.

## 29. Pay attention to her

Men may conquer cities and build empires, but remember this fact: women influence buying decisions. The end. Whether a mother and son, a wife and her husband, or a male attempting to impress a woman. Pay attention to the woman. In our post feminist society remember to appeal to the woman, get along, and respect her!

## 30. Ask names and ages

When you are really interested in others, success and favor occurs. When I play with other peoples kids I really mean it and enjoy it. Remember if you like their kids, they will see that you are interested in them. The key is: be genuine, celebrate family life.

## 31. Really be interested in them

It may seem redundant, but when you are talking to a future customer; focus all of your thought, intent, and energy towards the.

Connect

Spirit

Soul

And Body

They are the most important thing in your universe.

## 32. Value people

Now this is interesting. People = sales = $$$ in business. I am talking about valuing people in an affirming way. God in his infinite wisdom has put all types of folks on the earth. Learn to see the impact of everyone you meet. Esteem them highly, learn, and receive from them.

## 33. Talk F.A.B

Think of this as a commercial! When doing your 30 or 60 second commercial, talk:

Features . . . what it does

Advantages . . . why they want it

Benefits . . . why owning it will greatly enhance their life

Remember commercials inform, educate, and tickle the interest of future buyers. Pack your 30 or 60 seconds with F.A.B.

## 34. W.I.F.M

This truly is everyone's favorite radio station. We listen to "what's in it for me?" Explain what it will do for them. They want to know why and how they can obtain it. Always leave an opportunity for action.

## 35. Be joyful

People enjoy dealing with positive, happy, joyful, and upbeat people. Now you may not always feel that way, but put on a happy face and you will eventually get that way. Life is good. Act like it is. Practice joy, and joy comes.

## 36. Do not joke, unless you are the butt.

This sounds a little strange at first. Remember everyone is different, so are tolerances and sensitivity towards different things. Watch your joking with people. Some will love it, some will be offended. Always make yourself the butt of every joke. It's safer. Consider it Situational Awareness!

# 37. Blend like a chameleon

Always look for ways to fit into your
surroundings. Blend in, don't stick out.
We are most comfortable with people
like ourselves. Remember . . . don't wear
a suit to a rodeo. Jeans, cowboy boots,
and a hat will work nicely.

# 38. Think win/win

The win/win mindset is one of the most
powerful things to come along. If I get
what I want and win, and you get what
you want and win; our futures looks
promising. If I win and you lose, what do
you think that future looks like? Pretty
bleak.

## 39. Make people feel good

It's something we all crave, a good feeling. Good feelings create sales and allow people to spend money. Master the art of making people sincerely feel good and your success is guaranteed. Remember . . . many have been beaten down by criticism and rejection. We all respond to acceptance.

## 40. Bless people

Go out of your way to do good and bless people. You will be amazed how good you feel for doing this. Plant a good positive seed in the life of the people you meet and serve. Harvest time is inevitable. Genesis 8:22.

## 41. Be persistent

This works when nothing else does. Stay on task and keep talking and the law of averages will work for you. Stay steady and good things will come your way. Persistence pays. BE TENACIOUS !

## 42. Maintain a good work ethic

Show up on time. Work your shift. Be persistent. Stay on task. Leads will not fall on you like cherries from a tree. Work + effort = leads.

## 43. Stay relaxed

This will help you to work more
efficiently. Plus, people will respond
better to you if you stay that way.
Never get uptight when gathering leads.
Slow and steady wins the race! Run it
like a marathon. Have something at the
end.

## 44. Never sweat or fret

Make this the most natural thing you
can. When you get tight people will get
tight, sense danger and shut down. Keep
it real and natural. Keep your emotions in
check. Stay free and easy.

## 45. Detach emotions from the results

While emotional energy can help in the short run. A highly emotional effort is hard to maintain. I have found that a steady emotionally detached effort will yield the best, lasting results. You want to be in this for the long term. Stay steady!

## 46. Work the numbers

It's that simple! Totally! The more you ask, the more you will get. The percentage may vary, but if you ask enough people, some will say yes. See yourself as sorting through the numbers and you will become less frustrated.

## 47. Work the system

If you do not have one, please consider developing a system. This allows you to systematically work for leads—whether you feel good or bad, feel like it, or not. This is akin to developing a simple script. Oh so powerful. Oh so effective.

## 48. Ask for help

You most likely have a boss or supervisor. Ask questions, and ask for help. By doing this you are being teachable. Never get to the point where you think you know it all and do not need the help of others. No one succeeds alone.

# 49. Say please

As far as manners are concerned,
our world has taken a downward turn.
Watch in public places how we treat one
another. The one word that lubricates
all social interaction is PLEASE! Use the
word frequently and watch cooperation
increase in your life and business.

# 50. Say thank you

(Refer to # 49)

Thankfulness. Show gratitude. Be
grateful for what others do for you.
Your human relations will prosper.
Remember . . . little foxes spoil the
vines.

## 51. Don't work too hard

There is nothing worse than watching someone work too hard at generating leads. Usually these people are overachievers with big egos. Remember when you are all wired and jacked up, you will appear unnatural. People will become defensive. So relax, stay calm, and run your marathon.

## 52. Give emotionally to people

Learning to give of yourself to other people is profitable. So many are interested in only what "I" can get out of the deal. When you give from your heart to others you will feel good. And feeling good is good enough. What you give will come back to you. So give cheerfully.

# 53. Sow a loving, positive seed

If you look at the way this world is set up, you will find a principle. Seed time and Harvest, the positive seeds you plant in the lives of future customers—the more success you will have. Positive seeds = positive harvest. Negative seeds = negative harvest.

# 54. See yourself as a specialist

We all know our world is becoming highly specialized. See yourself as one. It takes certain definite skills to generate leads. Human relations skills, sales skills, and marketing skills. See yourself as a marketing professional. Everyone can't do what you do.

# 55. Envision success

Think, talk, see, and act nothing but
success. Believe in you and your product.
If you do this 100%, you will succeed.
See Victory before it happens.

# 56. Develop success rituals

A success ritual is an action you perform
that causes you to believe in your
success. For example: listen to a certain
song, use a clipboard, drink coffee, take
supplements, and even listen to success
and motivational tapes.

## 57. Laugh

Whatever you do, learn to laugh at yourself and interject humor into your relationships. Don't take yourself or your job too seriously. Highly motivated (good) can become driven or stressed (not good). Always look for humor in everyday life. Learn to laugh at YOURSELF.

## 58. Learn by experience

Let your experiences (or failures) be teachers and take knowledge from the experience. Experience, practice = learning, knowledge. Decide you will not quit and then decide that you never fail. All you are doing is practicing and gaining and learning knowledge. Awaken the winner.

## 59. Never think you have arrived

Not even for one minute. Pride and arrogance are really disguises for inferiority. Learn how to learn from every person and life experience. And please don't think you know it all. The smartest day of my life was when I turned 18. By 19 I had realized, I have a lot to learn. Become a lifelong learner.

## 60. Use giveaways

Nothing is more endearing than something for nothing. Many claim there is no free lunch. Nothing brightens your day like a freebie. So whatever you do use giveaways. Now the cost can be minimal, but give something of value to future customers.

## 61. Be flexible

We are all different, so remember to be flexible in your approach. What works at one venue may bomb at the next. Be adaptable to your environment. Be open to change. It separates a marketing pro from a wannabe.

## 62. Stay loose

The best way to get leads is to be relaxed and playful. The worst moments of days I have, are when I set high, unrealistic goals. This is a recipe for disaster. I push and strive and stress. People perceive that and do not respond to my offering. Stay loose, relaxed, and emotionally detached.

# 63. Think

This is something very few will do. Many people are followers and enjoy being told what to do. Leaders and winners learn to think through problems, adapt, and overcome. Dare to think you will be different than the multitudes. Be a self motivator.

# 64. Be a student of people

Learn from all the different types of people you meet. Be a student of human behavior. Don't fall for the old trap of "I can read people", until what they think comes out of their mouth. You don't know SQUAT! A jaded attitude will defeat you. I "know it all" will defeat you as well.

# 65. Listen

It's one of those skills we know about but . . . it really takes practice. Learn to do it with empathy and compassion, and mean it. People love good listeners. People will tell you what you need to know—if you listen. We are all looking for someone to share our journey with. What's in our hearts comes out our mouths.

# 66. Use time efficiently

Time is a commodity—do not waste it. Learning to manage it is a study in itself. When harvesting leads in the marketplace always remember that your time is valuable. Refuse to let anyone or anything waste it. Period. End of story.

# 67. Assume consent

Whenever presenting or offering anything (a card, giveaway, or premium) always believe people are interested in what you're offering. Assume and believe they are interested, and act accordingly. Your faith will make it happen. Belief is happening!

# 68. Reject rejection

Train your soul to reject rejection. After you have talked to 32 people and everyone says "no thanks", a normal human being will start thinking rejection. Relax, everyone feels it but winners train themselves not to be effected by it. Remember it is not you that people reject, but your offer.

## 69. Hyperextend your emotions

Sometimes, a high energy sprinter mentality will be the most effective way to achieve what you want. Use when necessary and pace yourself so you don't wear yourself out. Try pitching something for 1 hour. Learn when and how to turn it on!

## 70. Respond

Always know that unexpected things will come your way. Learn to respond from strength and principle as opposed to reacting emotionally. Reaction or response—the choice is yours. Now if you are prone to emotional reaction, be of good cheer. You can train yourself to respond from strength and logic.

## 71. Be well rested

Again, a common sense thought; but still important. The fresher and more alert you are, the better the response. Ever go somewhere and have a tired unenthusiastic employee attempt to serve you? People like dealing with upbeat folks!

## 72. Forget failure

Learn to forget failure the second it happens. When mistakes happen, learn from them and then forget it. Keep thinking about success and where you are going. The power of positive or negative thought works for everyone. Either attract, or repel success.

# 73. Laugh at yourself

Develop the habit of humor in life. Everything is not that important and you are not either. See humor in yourself and others. It is like medicine to your day. Laughter increases your sense of well being. With that, you master the day's challenges. Laugh often. Out loud. On purpose.

# 74. Remember faces

People are the most important thing to succeed in the sales and marketing profession. So remembering who you have talked to is invaluable. Faces, name, and occurrences all pay off richly. We all crave recognition in some form of another. Remember people.

## 75. Go towards them

Make your movements communicate.
Going towards the customer is an act
of inclusion. It says "I am interested
in you". Listen to what I have for you.
Make yo' motion profitable. This works in
all kinds of ways. Handshake, pat on the
back.

## 76. Expect success

Expect good to happen and come your
way and it will. Our life really is one big
self fulfilling prophecy with our beliefs
dictating our success and failures. You
really can if you think you can. Age old
platitudes but when really believed and
acted upon it yields results.

## 77. Eat right

I am still working on this one. But what we eat fuels our performance. Coke, Twinkies, and a Hershey bar will give you a sugar rush, but then the crash. Learn what fuels your body and eat right for you. I have found that protein works wonders and so do moderate carbs for me.

## 78. Move at their speed

The power of connection is priceless when gathering leads. So to enhance the process you need to move with people at their speed . . . we all like familiarity . . . . people are much more comfortable with like thinking like acting people . . . again it creates a current of favor that is hard to beat! And favor is what it's all about . . . a good lead generator relates to all kinds of people . . . at their pace and speed . . . a New Yorker to the guy from Brooklyn and a Texan to the man from Dallas . . . Connect, MOVE AT THEIR SPEED AND PACE!

## 79. Do not curse or use slang

Language is so beautiful and Words can be used so creatively . . . WHY? Lower yourself with vulgarity and slang . . . It just doesn't make sense. If you sound professional you will be treated as a professional. Remember you are selling you and your integrity . . . . use language for you and not against you! You will stand out from the crowd and that is your objection!

## 80. Let them win

There is nothing worse than being a person who always has to win in interpersonal relationships . . . let the other person win . . . learn to be self depreciating in your relationships . . . avoid the "type A tendency" to win at all costs . . . when others win we often do too! Sometimes losing is winning!

## 81. Be courteous & mannerly

Do you remember the phrase "mind your manners" . . . most likely coming from your mother . . . it really will be impressive when you remember to be courteous and mannerly in your dealings with others . . . in the world we live in it is a lost art . . . be sensitive to the needs of others and you will stand out in the crowd!

## 82. Focus totally

The Power of "undivided unbroken" Focus is immeasurable! Athletes and Artists know this intuitively . . . so should lead generators. The more you concentrate on doing one thing well the more success you will have . . . another simple concept . . . but can you do it? Remember . . . Focus on Them!

# 83. Demonstrate

A picture is worth a thousand words . . . act . . . demonstrate . . . be interactive . . . involve your customer . . . play . . . have fun . . . and for God's sake . . . Laugh . . . Joy is a powerful charismatic strength in the art of persuasion . . . Do it!

# 84. Play

When we went to school we had recess . . . we all enjoy recreation. Learn to put play and fun in your lead generating, people love to come out and play when allowed . . . the trouble is so much of us as adults forget what children know . . . make things fun . . . so be immature and let the heart of the child reinvigorate you in your work!

# 85. Be thankful

Living with a grateful heart is contagious . . . it can change and charge the atmosphere with confidence and success. Believe in your heart that interested buying people are coming your way . . . . they will show up! You can change YOUR world thru gratitude. Remember Thanksgiving? The Pilgrims knew something. WE still celebrate it every year.

# 86. Refuse discouragement

Resist this negative thought tenaciously . . . we all have highs and lows emotionally & physically . . . if tired get rest . . . weary in your soul reach out to someone and ride it out. This too shall pass! The feeling won't last! Remember people are interested in what you have!

# 87. Work with urgency

IT is important how you work. What you do will determine the success of your company. Believe in you and what you do. It really does matter. Others are depending on you. You are a catalyst to the World economy . . . and mainly yours. Your productivity changes the world economically!

# 88. Think others

The person who is wrapped up in themselves makes a small package. As a professional lead gatherer it is imperative that you think others first. Focus outwardly. About them . . . not what you want! What you give will come back to you. Remember others first!

# 89. Be gracious & endearing

See yourself as an ambassador of good will to the world . . . be willing to build rapport and be a nurturer of your customer. We all like to deal with warm people who are sincerely interested in us. THIS ONLY works when it is who you really are . . . . not a formula or a technique . . . people love to buy and hate being manipulated.

# 90. Be gentle & respectful

This is akin to 89! You really would be surprised though how you will stand out from your competitors when you have manners and actually treat people decent and with respect. So many today feel like they are doing you a favor by serving you. The customer still is King! Try going without them for a month???

# 91. Never . . . ever quit!

Quitters never win . . . so just don't do it. Take a break, regroup but never ever quit your goals and dreams in this life. Many quit just before they win. Quitters never win and winners never quit . . . Powerful words to live by!

You can if you want to bad enough! Never . . . ever . . . Never Quit!

# 92. Detest complacency

This one thing alone will cause success to follow you thru life as a professional lead generator. It is so easy to get complacent with this . . . it is doing one thing repetitively. Learn to detest it! Average is a place called mediocrity . . . true winners overcome it! ALWAYS!

## 93. Avoid self fulfilling prophecies

Perception is everything . . . You Can if you think you can. What we tell ourselves is what we believe. If we believe it long enough it will become true in our lives and manifest . . . Remember this formula thought + belief + words = our created reality . . . what we think and speak we will ultimately believe. Belief is HUGE! ENORMOUS!

## 94. Work peak times

Look at hunters and fishers . . . they always know the best times to hunt and fish. Work smart . . . not hard. The more traffic volume the better your chances . . . it's all in the numbers. Make them work for you!

## 95. Be realistic

While goal setting and PMA can accomplish a lot, be realistic in your expectations . . . setting unrealistic goals will always wear you out, frustrate and discourage you. Be realistic in your goals and assessments . . . you will do better, longer and much more successfully.

## 96. Hand them the pen

This is one of the oldest tips in the book . . . assume the consent or action you desire. Hand the pen to them. Lead those into it BELIEVE they are interested. This also applies to distributing literature or cards. ACT & BELIEVE! LEAD PEOPLE!

# 97. Display uniquely

Put life and a bit of enthusiasm in your display techniques. Dare to be a show off. Make the experience memorable and fun you will stand out from the crowd. Actually you are branding yourself to the consumer. Do and act unforgettable and you will never be forgotten!

# 98. Think marathon

Some leads are for immediate needs . . . some are not! Be a long term strategist and realize every lead gotten today will not sell next week or month. Keep the funnel full and something will come out. In my experience I have seen 10 year old leads generate sales!!! Be in it for the long haul . . . Think Marathon!

# 99. Don't take it all too seriously

Make this thing fun . . . enjoy playing with people to generate leads. My worst days happened when I got all tight and serious about this thing. Have fun . . . . act out a character . . . Enjoy yourself . . . Laugh . . . PLAY . . . STAY ON TARGET and you will succeed.

CONCLUSION. You have read . . . now practice and internalize . . . REFER TO THIS AS A REMINDER . . . give a copy to your friends and your enemies too. I would like to offer a special thank you to the following people who have helped me GROW along the way . . . bill & larry at peak marketing, sears, appleby systems, those remodeling guys . . . the history is yet to be written, david robinson, linda johnston, larry dessen, becky singh, john kailian, mark curry, warren lewis, tony beach, ryan boggs and jess black for helping with the manuscript. REMEMBER . . . . YOU MAKE IT HAPPEN!

I can be reached here@ bam357@ hotmail.com 717 370 1236 if you are in south central Pa. or Maryland AND Desire a garage makeover, refinished basement, organized closet or kitchen refacing go here. www. thoseremodelingguys.comAximum qui publicerum haliquam in Itam iam aurnum nonsul unum pata, C. Sat vent.

Sedo, mume nu seste terit; ervidemus conem, vere temurbis Cat, ut re que in

www.ingramcontent.com/pod-product-compliance
Lightning Source LLC
Chambersburg PA
CBHW021922170526
45157CB00005B/2139